SMALL FURRY ANIMALS

Rabbit

SMALL FURRY ANIMALS

Rabbit

Ting Morris

Illustrated by Graham Rosewarne

A+

Smart Apple Media

You see a tuft of gray-brown fur caught in the hedge and find holes in the ground. They look like little entrances, but who keeps the grass around them so short? Surely no one mows the grass in this field?

4

Just as you're wondering who made the holes,
two long ears pop out of one of them.

Turn the page and take a closer look.

A little rabbit hops onto the grass and starts nibbling away. He's followed by three more pairs of long ears. These youngsters belong to a colony of rabbits that live underground. The rabbits are just four weeks old, but they can already look after themselves. They come out to eat when it starts to get dark, but for safety they stay close to the burrow entrance. If anything startles them, they bolt back down.

LONG-EARED HISTORY

Rabbits like these originally lived in Spain and northern Africa. From there they spread throughout Europe, and people eventually took them to every continent in the world except Antarctica. They live wild in many regions and have also become popular pets.

6

Cottontails

Cottontails are wild rabbits found in North and South America. They are named for their short, fluffy tails, which look like balls of cotton. Although they are very similar to other rabbits, cottontails don't live in groups.

WHAT ARE MAMMALS?

All rabbits and hares are mammals. A mammal has hair or fur on its body to help keep it warm. Baby mammals are fed with milk from their mother's body. Human beings are mammals, too.

Rabbit or hare?

Hares are bigger than rabbits and have longer ears. You can tell the difference between the two when they run away from danger. A rabbit moves its tail up and down, flashing the white fur underneath. Hares keep their tails down, showing the dark top side, and flatten their ears for speed.

Something must have frightened the four young rabbits. Perhaps they heard or smelled you. Look at them racing along the tunnels—they certainly know their way around. The rabbits' underground home is a maze of tunnels and rooms, with many entrances and exits. The top, or dominant, rabbits always live in the best rooms, and youngsters respect them and stay out of their way.

The warren

Rabbits may make their underground home, called a warren, in fields, hedgerows, sand dunes, sea cliffs, or along railroad tracks. The warren's tunnels, which are often called burrows, are all connected. Some are dead ends, where rabbits can hide if an enemy such as a weasel or ferret gets into the warren. Other burrows are escape hatches.

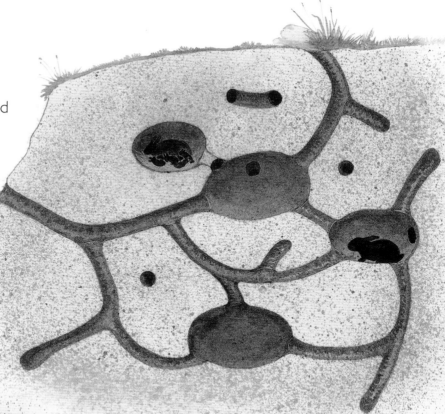

Smooth burrows

The burrow entrance is about six inches (15 cm) wide, with the grass nibbled away along the edge and bare earth around it. The soil inside the burrow is smooth, because the rabbits brush it all the time with their fur.

FEMALE BUILDERS

All burrows are dug by female rabbits. They scrape away the soil with their front feet, push it away with their hind legs, and chew through any roots that are in the way. The warren may be up to 10 feet (3 m) deep, so this takes a lot of work.

9

On this moonlit night, all the rabbits are out feeding. Can you spot the youngsters? Out in the field, the top rabbits get the best food and nibble on the sweetest plants. Adult males don't just eat during this time, though. They also mark their home patch to show who's boss. It's a warning to young bucks in the colony not to get too bold, and it keeps the neighbors away. Rabbits from other warrens know by the smell that this territory has already been claimed.

TOP LIVING QUARTERS

Rabbits live in family groups of between 12 and 30 adults. The colony is ruled by a strict status system called a hierarchy, and the dominant males and females (the strongest and most aggressive rabbits in the colony) live in the best part of the warren, the middle. Top bucks pair up with top does, and their offspring will also be strong.

Chinning

Male rabbits rub the ground with their chin to mark their home patch. They have special glands under the chin that secrete a yellow, scented liquid. If a dominant buck sniffs a scent mark made by a weaker rabbit, he puts his own scent over it.

LIVING ON THE EDGE

The lowest-ranking and weakest rabbits live at the edge of the warren. This is the most dangerous place, because an enemy intruder will attack the first rabbit it finds.

The rabbit warren is near the edge of a field, close to lots of tasty grains and juicy plant shoots. A little bit of bark makes a crunchy snack between meals. One of the rabbits has discovered a vegetable patch with carrots and cabbages, but unfortunately, it's just out of bounds. The edges of their territory are clearly marked with scrapes and droppings. You can see rabbit droppings around the tree stump and on the anthill—they look like brown peas.

12

WHAT'S FOR LUNCH?

In the spring and summer, rabbits enjoy green leafy plants, grass, clover, herbs, and grains. In winter, they make do with twigs, bark, and seeds. When feeding, a rabbit moves around in a circle with its face close to the ground. Rabbits can cause great damage to crops and trees.

Scrapes

Scrapes are bare patches of soil in the grass. Rabbits make them around their warren to mark their territory. Because territories are clearly marked, rabbits from different warrens rarely fight.

WHAT'S FOR DESSERT?

After feeding, rabbits rest all day in their burrows and eat the soft droppings of their half-digested food. This doesn't sound very appetizing, but these first droppings are full of vitamins and minerals. The droppings you see on the ground are the second, dry ones.

Droppings

Rabbits leave droppings around the edges of their home patch. Their communal latrines are usually on a high place, such as a tree stump or an anthill, where they can be seen by neighboring warrens. These high places also make good lookout points.

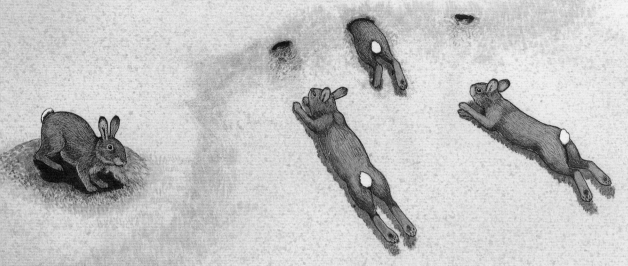

All rabbits enjoy sunbathing. But daytime feeding is risky, and rabbits are constantly watching and listening for danger. There's a hawk high up in the air, circling the field. The hunter has chosen its victim—a young rabbit half asleep in the sunshine. A lookout spots the enemy and thumps the ground to warn the others. But it's too late for the drowsy sunbather. As the hawk swoops down on its prey, the young rabbit gives out a piercing scream—a last warning signal.

Fighting fit

Rabbits have powerful legs, and a healthy, full-grown rabbit is almost impossible to catch. When frightened, a rabbit can leap 10 feet (3 m) and race as fast as 25 miles (40 km) per hour in hops and zigzags. If attacked, it kicks with its hind legs and bites with its sharp teeth. But rabbits usually try to hide or sit as still as a statue, hoping they have not been noticed.

ALARM SIGNALS

To warn others in the colony of danger, rabbits thump the ground with their hind feet. When they run away, their tail bobs up and down, and the white underside acts as an alarm signal. Rabbits are quiet animals, but they scream if they are caught, giving an extra warning to the others.

Eyes and ears

When rabbits move their long ears, they can pick up sounds from any direction. Their ears also make a useful fan in the heat. A rabbit's eyes are on the side of its head, toward the back, so it can see in all directions at once and spot an enemy coming from behind.

15

These two rabbits are a couple. The doe's mate is a big, strong buck—can you tell which is which? During their courtship, the couple stay close to each other, feeding, sleeping, and grooming together. Soon the doe will prepare a nursery den for her babies. It will be her first litter, and she'll have many more within the next year.

Bath time

Rabbits keep their fur clean by washing and grooming regularly, especially early in the evening. They use their tongue, teeth, and claws to wash their face, ears, and feet. During courtship, grooming becomes a joint exercise, and rabbits lick their partner's fur.

BREEDING SEASON

Rabbits are ready to mate when they are between three and four months old. A female rabbit is pregnant for 28 to 30 days. Between February and August, she can have one litter per month, each with five to six young. Many young rabbits die in their first year.

Nursery burrow

Before giving birth, the mother prepares her nursery den. She digs a special tunnel between three and six feet (1–2 m) long. The nursery burrow is a dead end, and there she builds a nest that she lines with grass and her own fur.

ive helpless baby rabbits are asleep in their nest. They are just two days old and are blind, deaf, and hairless. Every night, their mother comes into the nursery to feed her young. The kittens suck her milk, but they must be quick because she stays only for a few minutes. The mother rabbit is in a hurry because she needs to continue eating. After nursing, the doe blocks the entrance to the nursery den with earth. This keeps heat in and enemies out.

COTTONTAIL'S NEST

The female cottontail digs a shallow nest in the ground, hidden by tall grass. She stays near the nest and covers her babies with grass and fur to keep them warm and hide them from enemies.

18

Kittens

At birth, baby rabbits weigh just over one ounce (30 g). Their mother suckles them for three weeks, and they grow quickly on her rich milk. By the time they are eight days old, they have more than doubled in weight and can see and hear. They have fluffy fur and are ready to go on little explorations in the burrow.

Good teeth

Rabbits' teeth grow constantly throughout their lives. The front teeth are as sharp as chisels. Rabbits have two pairs of upper incisors, one behind the other. There's a big gap between the front teeth and the back teeth, or molars. The molars are ridged and are used to grind food.

An enemy has smelled the kittens, sneaked through the burrows, and broken into the nursery. The mother rabbit is away, and there's no one to help the young. The weasel snatches the smallest rabbit and sneaks out as quietly as it came. What will the mother do when she visits her babies tonight? Will she notice that one is missing?

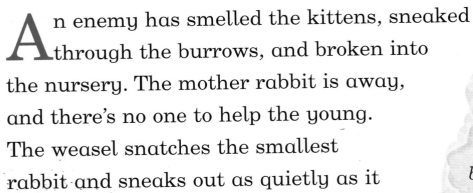

RABBIT CATCHERS

People are a rabbit's greatest enemy. This is because rabbits are seen as pests by farmers, foresters, and gardeners. Some people also hunt rabbits for food.

Natural enemies

Many different animals hunt rabbits for food: foxes, coyotes, badgers, weasels, ferrets, snakes, hawks, owls, eagles, and other birds of prey. In the wild, rabbits usually live no longer than three years.

badger

owl

hawk

weasel

snake

coyote

fox

Hop on board

Explorers used to take wild rabbits with them across the oceans and leave them on islands to provide food for later voyages. Just over 100 years ago, 24 rabbits were taken to Australia from Europe, and before long, there were millions of them. They ate so much grass that Australians decided to set traps and infect the rabbits with a deadly disease to stop them from spreading any further.

MYXOMATOSIS

Myxomatosis is a viral disease that was used to keep the rabbit population down in France. In the 1950s, a doctor infected a pair of rabbits with the virus, which is passed on by fleas. Young rabbits pick up their first fleas from their mothers, and the fleas are then passed around the warren.

21

By late summer, the warren is getting overcrowded. All the nurseries are full of babies, and the grass is getting eaten faster than it can grow. The older bucks and does are defending their patch and forcing the younger rabbits to the edge of the warren. Young females have had to dig their breeding burrows far away from the main warren.

LITTER GAMES

Young rabbits play with each other and have pretend fights when they leave the nursery burrow. The games are not just for fun—they are also a way of finding out who is strongest.

22

Swamp rabbits

In the United States, from Georgia to Texas, lives a strange kind of rabbit called a swamp rabbit. Swamp rabbits are excellent swimmers and divers, which is useful when they are being chased. They live under logs or in hollows in the ground.

NO ROOM IN THE WARREN

When the rabbit population gets too big, the older, dominant rabbits become aggressive, and weak rabbits are pushed right out of the warren. The homeless are easy prey for enemies and soon die. Strong young rabbits begin to dig new burrows and start their own colony.

Pets

The European or common rabbit is the ancestor of tame, domesticated rabbits. These pets are kept in a special cage called a hutch. They grow bigger and fatter than their wild relatives, and their fur is longer and more colorful. Pet rabbits may be black, brown, gray, or spotted.

The young rabbit you first saw pop out of the burrow is the strongest among his group, and they are starting up their own warren. They are using an abandoned nursery burrow as the start of their new home. Fast diggers are tunneling day and night, and they have certainly chosen a good place. The new warren will be right under the vegetable patch that used to be out of bounds. The rabbits will live through the winter on juicy carrots and cabbages. Next spring, this patch will be a playground with lots of rabbits hopping about.

WINTERTIME

Rabbits don't like cold and snow. To keep warm, a rabbit needs to eat more, but finding food beneath the snow is difficult. During a cold spell, rabbits usually stay in the warren until hunger drives them out. In severe winters, only the strongest survive.

Locked out

Farmers who want to protect their vegetables and crops from nibbling rabbits have to put up special rabbit-proof fencing. This fencing goes down about 28 inches (70 cm) below the ground and all around the vegetable patch.

Pikas

Pikas are related to rabbits, but they look more like guinea pigs with their short, rounded ears and tailless bottoms. They live in colonies in the mountains of North America and Asia. These clever little creatures gather grass in the summer and use it for food during the winter.

25

RABBIT CIRCLE OF LIFE

Pregnant females dig special nursery tunnels at the edge of the warren. They have between three and five litters a year.

Rabbits mate mainly in the spring and summer. In a colony, dominant males pair up with dominant females.

Rabbits are fully grown when they are about four months old.

Mother rabbits suckle their young at night.

When they are three weeks old, youngsters begin going outside to graze.

Young rabbits become independent and leave the nursery burrow when they are a month old.

Glossary

buck A male rabbit.

burrow A rabbit's tunnel.

colony A large group of animals that live close together as a community.

den An animal's home or resting place.

doe A female rabbit.

dominant Strongest or most aggressive.

glands Organs inside the body that produce important substances.

groom To clean the fur or skin.

hierarchy A system in which animals are ranked according to their strength or importance.

hind leg Back leg.

kitten A young rabbit.

litter A number of baby animals born at one time.

mate When a male and female animal come together to make babies.

nursery den A den where an animal cares for its young.

offspring An animal's young.

pregnant With young developing inside the body.

prey An animal that is killed and eaten by another animal.

suckle To feed milk to a young animal.

territory The area that an animal defends against animals of the same kind, to keep them away.

warren A network of rabbit burrows.

INDEX

31

Published by Smart Apple Media
2140 Howard Drive West, North Mankato, Minnesota 56003

Designed by Helen James
Illustrated by Graham Rosewarne

Photographs by Corbis (Tom Bean, D. Robert & Lorri Franz,
Darrell Gulin, Kelly-Mooney Photography, Joe McDonald),
Jim Brandenburg/Minden Pictures

Printed and bound in Thailand

Library of Congress Cataloging-in-Publication Data

Morris, Ting.
Rabbit / by Ting Morris.
p. cm. — (Small furry animals)
Includes index.
ISBN 1-58340-521-6
1. Rabbits—Juvenile literature. [1. Rabbits.] I. Title. II. Small furry animals
(Mankato, Minn.)

QL737.L32M67 2004
599.32—dc22   2003067252

First Edition

9 8 7 6 5 4 3 2 1